RIGHT-FIT DIGITAL STRATEGY TO ACCELERATE GROWTH

11-Elements Digital Adoption Framework for your Organization

Anirvan Sen

5C Digital Innovation Series

ISBN: 9798655790711

I would like to dedicate this book to my father, Dr Bimal Kanti Sen, who started my inspirational education journey and who continues to enthuse me with his ideas.

CONTENTS

INTRODUCTION

This is the decade when most businesses will become digital. It does not matter whether you are a logistics business, a training company, a retail business or a consulting business, most of the activities of your company are going to be conducted on a digital medium.

Interacting with customers, collaborating on your project, coaching your remote teams, measuring performance as well as coffee machine discussions will be done using collaboration platforms like MS Teams, Zoom, social media, digital funnels, email exchanges and VR platforms. It won't be too long before we will have virtual board meetings using VR devices that will make us feel as if we are physically sitting together.

However, businesses across the world believe that in-order to become digital they must acquire massive technology capabilities. These capabilities would include programming in Natural Programming Language, ability to mine big data and have data scientists, should have quants in their teams who can look at complex problems, and seamlessly structure details to get value-added knowledge. And the list goes on and on.

In-light of these requirements, what do you think an average business owner, or a senior operational manager of a non-native digital company would do? They would look at their core, and they would go "If it ain't broke, don't fix it". And they would get back to their desks and focus on other business priorities.

But the world is changing. More people are getting on to the digital band wagon. 4+ billion people are active online and more than half of them access social media platforms like Facebook, Instagram, WhatsApp and other programs on a regular basis. This is leading to fundamental shifts in the way businesses get conducted. One does not have to look far. If you were to look at Top-20 Fortune 500 companies in the late 20th century and compare it with the current list, the difference is starkly visible with several digital companies now being part of the list.

With so many people being online and companies adopting novel ways to connect with customers and even prospective buyers using enabling technologies, it has become imperative that all businesses must have a digital strategy. It does not matter whether it is a technology company, a digital company, a brick-and-mortar store or a utilities company, in order to survive in the future everybody needs to think digital.

But how do I become digital?

Most businesses struggle with this conundrum. Even with a good understanding of enabling technologies, businesses fight with finding the right applications within their organization. The bridge between theory and relevance is often a bridge too far.

But innovation always finds its way through. The COVID-19 crisis exactly did that. It accelerated the need for businesses to become digital.

Necessity is the mother of all inventions.

So, where do you start?

Digital adoption is a journey and like any journey, it needs to start with awareness. This is precisely the approach, we at Fifth Chrome have taken. While there is a place to understand the technical parts of the digital world, we firmly believe that the real power of these enabling technologies is to unleash their ability to solve complex business problems and create wonderfully new ways to conducting business.

That is why our digital education journey also, starts with the basic awareness on how different business problems can be solved by adopting digital and more importantly, how can going digital help your business to grow exponentially. Only after getting a good foundational understanding, do we recommend our participants to proceed to more advanced and erudite levels.

The essence of this book is to prepare your business to embark on a digital journey. Digital adoption is not a binary step for a company. Instead, it is made up of several steps taken together. We have tried to explain concepts in a simple and non-technical way so that it can be easily understandable for every reader.

Our own approach has been to use listen-and-reflect during our training and workshops. We have extended the same philosophy in this book as read-and-reflect. And to help you with this, we have included checklists of questions at the end of each chapter.

This book will provide you a structured approach on how to adopt digital technology seamlessly and unlock opportunities that will put your business on a high growth trajectory.

Last but not the least, digital adoption is likely to provide you much more benefit than you can ever dream of. The trick is being open enough to change and then let the digital work its magic.

I wish you all the best in your digital journey and hope you can create some real path-breaking value for your organizations.

This book is part of a series. More details can be found at our website www.fifthchrome.com. Please visit us to learn more about our books, our workshops and training, as well as resources that we regularly share including tips, templates and expert interviews.

To ask technical questions or to contact, send us an email at info@fifthchrome.com. Just mention the book name in the subject line so it lands with the right team.

POWERING EXPONENTIAL GROWTH

Workplace technology has gone through an accelerated evolution over the last couple of decades. Starting from the personal computer as a box that sat on your desktop, every one now has a hundred times more powerful device like a smartphone sitting in our pockets. This accelerated evolution in its initial stages was primarily designed to offer faster, cheaper, better and more efficient ways of doing things but if you look at the last decade, you will see that this accelerated evolution was actually a digital revolution. Industry after industry is being disrupted by new and innovative ways of doing business. We do not have to look far for examples.

Uber, founded in 2009, completely disrupted the cab industry world over. Not just that, uberization has emerged as a word that is increasingly being adopted in the business world whenever people refer to a platform that is created based on hundreds of small business owners and individuals. Another example to illustrate the point is Airbnb. Another disruptive company that challenged the behemoth of a strongly controlled hospitality industry. By bringing in spare capacity of many homes, combining it with beautiful photography and amplified user experience, Airbnb rewrote the rulebook of the travel industry. These two examples show that digital technology changes over the last decade have been nothing short of a revolution.

By embracing enabling technologies, millions of companies have emerged all over the world. But how about the businesses that have a physical presence with physical products, services, software, or human capital? Can they become digital and compete in the digital economy?

And the emphatic answer is Yes.

Not only these businesses can become digital and compete, but they are running out of time if they do not get onto the digital bandwagon soon. The COVID-19 crisis showed this truth in a very ugly way. So many companies simply got wiped out in a matter of months because they did not think digital.

What is interesting is that, not only digital can be a great business add-on, digital technologies can enable organizations to setup separate divisions and even businesses that can grow your business. The icing on the cake is that by skillfully adopting digital technologies and thinking, businesses can accelerate their growth exponentially.

In this chapter, we will explore various rationales why it makes strategic sense for any brick-&-mortar business to adopt digital technologies and create hyper-growth capabilities. These rationales have been categorized into 8 factors:
- Fast
- Cheap
- Market access
- Agility
- Latent market
- Network effect
- Scale-up
- Democratization

Fast

Fast can be described from two different angles. One is the

speed of processing data or information. Secondly, it is the speed by which businesses can adopt digital technologies, software, and platforms.

Digital technologies offer machine computing power that is far superior to human computing power. Therefore, if you are in the business of providing a service and have components that are repeatable and have mainly rule-based activities, then you have a chance to convert this into a digital service. Once these activities are converted into digital services, these activities will get done in a jiffy.

Let us say, part of your service is to onboard every new client. This onboarding exercise includes one of your associates filling a series of forms through a physical discussion. Usually, to do this exercise, your client, and your associate need to agree upon a date and time when they can meet. What if by streamlining your on-boarding process, you can digitize your set of activities through an online platform, imagine the amount of time, effort as well as physical interventions can be eliminated, and thus saving your company valuable time of your associate as well as removing the waiting-time waste.

In the past, it was all about computing power. Now, with machine learning and artificial intelligence, faster computing has been given a brain as well. Not only can you perform activities much faster but many of the contextual human judgements are being replaced by robots. Robotics process automation or RPA as it is popularly known, is replacing jobs in finance, HR, logistics, supply-chain, marketing, and many other spheres of an organization.

And then there are new technologies, that for the first time, have given us the ability to mine gargantuan amounts of data and that too, in quick time to get valuable insights about our consumers, users and the market in general. We can in real-time, understand the behavior of potential customers and perform spot-pricing to lure them to purchase our goods. Thus, providing a tremendous advantage to your business. We have digital solutions now that are based on weather conditions, that can change and control irrigation for your crops as well as maintain humidity in your greenhouses.

Cheap

Another significant advantage of digital is its related costs. After the industrial revolution, only mega-rich could afford to create businesses. Each new business would need significant amount of capital expense in terms of land, machinery, inventories, and fees for setup. The only exception were businesses that were centered around specific craft and skills of individuals. Even for them, the need of capital was still paramount. Even government agencies would charge an exorbitant fee and expect you to have a minimum amount of capital available for investment. This kept the ability of creating a new business, out of reach for most people.

Digital technologies have changed all of that. Today, it is possible for anybody with an idea and a laptop to setup a business with almost no cash required. Places like Singapore would charge 1 SGP to setup a business.

The technology scenario has changed significantly. Back in the 80s and 90s, one would need to spend thousands to get a desktop and relevant software. Now, with cloud-computing, and with software-as-a-service, many basic features of software are available for free and power models start with less than a $20 monthly payment option.

Consider this. You can buy your business name domain for less than $10 and have it hosted under $100 per year. With WordPress, you can easily manage to create a professional looking website by yourself. Or through sites like Upwork, you can hire freelancers to create a website in less than a few hundred dollars in a matter of days. Setting up your own business online has never been cheaper.

If your business is centered around a smartphone app then some of the basic apps can be developed under $10k. Imagine if you and three of your friends got together and spent a few months of time and effort to develop a new app, from your uncle's garage, the only cost that you incurred was for endless bags of chips and pizzas. The best part of the news is that both you and your friends used your spare capacity during the evenings and the weekends to create the app.

This is the power of digital technologies being made available for a fraction of a cost of setting up a conventional business in the past.

Market Access

Before the digital commerce age, most businesses would start by selling their products and services locally. Once they gained in size and revenue only then they would venture beyond their locations, to expand their business.

There are more than 4.5 online users and more than 2 billion people use social media platforms like Facebook, WhatsApp, LinkedIn, Twitters, and Instagram actively. If you develop a digital product or an online app, you immediately get access to thousands of people and if your product have international features then you can serve millions of potential consumers from all over the world in no time.

And what are these international features? Sites being in English language, products with universal appeal like music, education, games. As you can see, you do not need sophisticated products to access these international waters. Even with simple concepts you can reach people across the globe. You can setup your own YouTube channel and you can have people following you from across the globe.

Look at food bloggers like Mark Wiens (6+ million subscribers) or Trevor James (4+ million subscribers) who have created monetization mechanisms through their food vlog on YouTube. Their subscribe base is from across the globe.

Agility

Due to low development costs, quick deployment ability, and immediate access to thousands of users, businesses can get instant feedback from the market with digital products and services.

This ability not only provides meaningful market insights but also, allows the businesses to make quick changes and then redeploy the product. Digital platforms provide agility to quickly change and in more serious cases, pivot your business without significant investments.

If your digital marketing campaign receives a tepid response, you can quickly decide to either tweak it or in some cases shelve it. In fact, companies use concepts like A/B testing (two variations of a campaign are launched to see which does better than the other) from the start to gain a better traction in the market.

The other flexibility of relatively cheaper costs and high-speed of deployment, gives organizations the ability to conduct multiple experiments in the market to connect with users and customers. By constantly and consistently conducting hundreds of experiments, companies can continuously learn and improve their products, services as well as their interactions with their consumers.

Fail fast, learn faster is the new motto for many digital businesses.

Latent Market

In the pre-internet days, companies used to develop products and services that had mass appeal. These products and services were developed keeping an average user in mind. One-glove-fit-all approach worked for most businesses. Even consumers got used to having just a few options. But the digital age changed it all.

Michael Dell is one of the first businessmen who pioneered the concept of customized product and services. Whether he drew his inspiration from custom-made pizzas or not, I cannot say that, but giving the customers an ability to choose and customize their PCs was a revolutionary thinking. Some customers needed bigger data storage space whereas others needed voluminous data crunching abilities, Dell computers now made it possible for both these customers to be served with the same product line.

With digital commerce, the level of customization has been taken to a whole new level. Consumers who were part of a long tail-end of a market graph, can now have their requirements satiated by specific products and services. This is known as micro-niche.

So, if your business has an idea that caters to a certain demography, with a certain taste, and a certain income, who like certain services, at a certain cost, with certain flexibilities, and the list goes on…, with digital platforms you can easily reach this micro-niche and serve them.

Look at McDonalds that is running a campaign with vegetable chicken burgers or Dominos pizzas offering gluten-free pizzas, these businesses have been able to identify and address the micro-niche demands based on data analytics.

Consultants and trainers can create digital products specifically for micro-niche. Khan's Academy is a perfect example of how an organization combined the latent needs of millions of schoolchildren across the globe with the advances of technology, to create a training platform to provide high-quality education, in a simple-to-understand format that is now used across the globe.

Not just that. Digital products can now reach your non-customers, refusing customers and even people who were completely unaware of your products easily. By creating digital marketing funnels, you can tailor-make campaigns addressing each of these specific crowd and then capturing every single digital interactions from these groups to understand their needs and wants much better than you could ever do in the past. With better understanding, you can now customize your product and target these groups with a lot more confidence and woo the market.

Network Effect

Network effect is a distinctive phenomenon of the digital

world. As the number of consumers grow, the value of your product or platform grows. And that in turn, gets more consumers creating a positive feedback loop.

So, when you launch a digital product and you can get traction with your consumers, your consumers will end up discussing your product with their network and share your details, which will lead to more people coming to use your product and that starts a positive spiral. For products that get good traction, it creates a buzz in the market. This buzz can send hundreds of potential customers your way, without necessarily creating an expensive marketing campaign.

By engaging social media platforms like Instagram, Facebook, Twitter and LinkedIn, digital businesses try to create buzz with their products and offers regularly.

Scale

With cheap software, crowdsourced development team, pay-as-you-go services, and cloud-computing, you can potentially scale any digital product massively. This is a true power of digital products.

Think of an eBook or a digital training video. You can create thousands of copies for almost no cost and then distribute them in no time to potential clients without emptying your bank.

You can create millions of copies of your software and sell them now without thinking of assembly lines, warehouses, and inventory management.

With little investment, you can exponentially scale your product distribution that was never possible with a physical product in the past.

Democratization

Enabling technologies and digital platforms are massive field levelers. For the first time in human history, every person with an idea has now the ability to setup a business anywhere in the world, almost anywhere. With government supported initiatives and digital innovations-on-steroid, it has never been as easy as it is today to develop your product and businesses with truly little capital.

This is the true democratization of the business world.

As we step into the 2020s, massive developments are taking place in the technology world. Virtual reality, Blockchain, Artificial Intelligence, Cloud-computing, Big-Data, IoT and human-machine interfaced applications are creating millions of new products and services. These developments will continue to disrupt industry after industry.

Many businesses are at cross-roads on their plans about digital adoption. The worst part is that there are still a large number of businesses that refuse to acknowledge the power of digital disruption. It is these businesses that I am worried about.

The reality is the next digital revolution has already started. Now is the time for you to decide whether to embrace the new digital order and be a Digital Fortuna or get deluged and fade into obscurity by the Digital Tsunami.

◆ ◆ ◆

Checklist 1: Digital Empowerment Baseline

This is a checklist to conduct a preliminary baseline of your company's current digital state.

1. Does your business have any digital product or service?
2. Does your business have a specific digital strategy?
3. Has your leadership team evaluated how enabling technologies can be used in the business?
4. Does your leadership team know specific areas where these enabling technologies can be deployed?
5. Does your website generate leads on a regular basis?
6. Does your business have presence in social media?
7. Does your business conduct email campaigns, and track

and actionize individual user interaction with the emails?

8. Can you show evidence where your social media presence has directly created revenue for you?

9. How do you digitally create awareness about your products and services?

10. Does your company embark on digital marketing with a funnel approach to woo potential customers?

11. Does your company do content marketing?

12. Does your company publish specific white papers, blogs, and case studies related to your businesses experience and insight, with a high frequency apart from generic content marketing (at least 1-2 times every month)?

13. Do you capture and deep analyze all digital interactions with your customers and prospects?

14. What is the state of your competitor's digital adoption?

15. What is the state of your supplier, customer, and your partner's digital presence?

BUSINESS TRENDS

As we enter the 2020s, we are going to witness unprecedented changes in the business world. We started the decade with the COVID-19 crisis that is crippling the world trade and economy in so many ways. Many businesses will be affected badly and will never be able to come out of it. On the other hand, digital technology has rapidly evolved over the last 10 years and we are going to witness their true power being unleashed during this decade. The baby boomers who were considered the loyalist generation, are set to retire from the active workforce in the coming decade. And during the same time, we will witness many of the Gen-Z join the work force.

Many of these trends will have significant impact on the world economy. For our purposes, I have identified six trends that I believe will play a defining role in the business world that has a direct connection with digital technology. These trends are:

- Baby boomers and Gen-X approaching retirement
- Covid-19 defining a new normal
- Rapid technology advances
- Millennials and Gen-Z's influence on work culture
- International and Cross-border trade
- Deconstruction of jobs

Baby-Boomers And Gen-X Approaching Retirement

Most of the developed world is moving towards an ageing population and the median age is constantly moving higher. This includes countries in Western Europe, US, Japan and even China. This is because most baby-boomers will be 65 or older by 2030 and likely to retire in the coming decade if they have not already done so by now.

With advances in medicine and healthcare, people now will live longer than their previous generation. When I was a child, I could not remember seeing a lot of people who were older than 90 years. But now when I look at the same age group, I see a lot more people in that population group.

This trend is bringing in some economic challenges for the individual countries. In general, older people need more medicines and access to healthcare systems. Therefore, we will see an increased dependency of this group on state funds, pensions and other financial subsidies related to healthcare systems. Secondly, as the age median go higher, there will be less people in the workforce to be able to support the government coffers and tax systems. These factors are going to strain the exchequers of most governments.

So, these governments would be desperately looking for answers to their problems. One of the areas, where they will look at, is digital and technology innovation. We are likely to witness a surge in big data analytics and artificial intelligence-based healthcare solutions. AI-based diagnostics, preventive healthcare and robot-based monitoring are few examples of initiatives in this space.

Covid-19 Defining A New Normal

The current pandemic has cast a long shadow to the business world across the world. Global supply-chains have been interrupted, physical interactions have been severely limited, and lockdowns have only allowed vital services to continue. How long will this continue, what level of devastation will this crisis leave behind and when will the economies bounce back, only time will tell.

We can however, with confidence say that two phenomena will take place.

First is that we will have a "New Normal" way of leading our lives just as we had after Hurricane Katrina, 9/11 and SARS outbreak.

Second, acceleration of digital adoption like never seen before. In fact, this one has already started, and we will see massive surge in the coming few months. More transactions are going to be done online and through digital medium. People would be averse to traveling soon and will maintain some social distance and, in many instances, telecommute and work remotely. This will hugely increase the dependency on digital platforms.

Unfortunately, most businesses are woefully unprepared to adopt digital technology in quick time and even those, who adopt them quickly are unable to unleash the exceptional opportunities because of faulty adoption.

There were companies prior to the crisis that had adopted some levels of digital technology in their organization albeit reluctantly. Much of their leadership were nay-sayers and skeptics of digital technology. That is why, many of them just decided to open a digital channel but not really focus on it. They chose to continue their focus on main line of business. Ironically, the current crisis completely changed their thinking and overnight changed them to promoters of digital innovation.

But there are just a few of these lucky ones. Even for these companies, had they implemented digital the right way, they would be reaping the benefits of exceptional growth.

What most people do not realize is that the digital medium not only provides an alternate medium to conduct business in, it provides a massive number of opportunities that can be unleashed to provide exponential growth.

Like any other transformational change, every large-scale change needs a compelling reason to trigger the transformation. For the digital world that was lurking as a low plan B option for many companies, the current crisis has just provided that massive compelling reason for companies to transform and to adopt digital technology earnestly.

Rapid Technology Advances

We have witnessed unparalleled growth in technology in the last 10 years. This trend is only going to accelerate in the coming decade. We will increasingly witness technology entering spaces that we have not seen before.

Artificial intelligence is going to be extensively used in the healthcare system for diagnostics. In fact, we already see artificial intelligence being used heavily in medical imaging and healthcare applications. These AI engines have far better accuracy in identifying and predicting illnesses like cancer than human beings can. AI is also going to be used for targeted marketing, inventory management, recruitment, and sophisticated business processes like dynamic pricing.

Blockchain adoption as a multiparty system is going to gain traction specially in the areas of supply chain and logistics. We are going to see more collaboration between multiple parties, consortiums and other associations being formed to reap benefits of using multiparty system. Blockchain is going to tremendously increase the transparency in a supply chain and thus, attacking counter feeds and fraud problems with strong veracity.

5G technology is being rolled out across the globe. When we combined the power of 4G and smart phones, it gave rise to the technological advances that we witness in the last decade. Uber, Airbnb, Netflix, and social media platforms, all benefitted from the power of 4G. Imagine what kind of innovation is 5G likely to bring to our lives. Usage of voice-based devices, autonomous driving, and VR based apps, will all get hugely benefited by the power of 5G.

Immersive media is yet another technology manifestation that is going to enter our lives much more prominently in this decade. VR, AR and 360° videos are going to be introduced in an affordable and usable manner. Whether conducting board meetings remotely, traveling to a virtual island for an experience or visually inspecting to lease an apartment, you will be using your smart phone with 5G.

These are just few examples from the tons of exciting things that are happening in the world of technology.

Millennials And Gen-Z Workforce

Most of the millennial's are already in the workforce and Gen-Z has started joining as well. These two generations have grown up with technology. For many of them, it is difficult to comprehend the world before Google or Facebook. This is the digitally native generation.

This generation is hardwired to think differently compared to baby boomers and Gen X. They use digital devices with the same alacrity as the previous generations used pen and paper. Taking photos and videos that was considered a novelty for the previous generation, has now been deeply integrated with the daily lives of this generation. Posting photos on Instagram and Facebook a few times in a day is quite common amongst this group. They are also very adept in searching for information online and using their social network to get answers for the challenges they may face.

As this group becomes a bigger part of the workforce, they will bring in their de facto digital thinking to their work.

Moreover, unlike their prior generations that lived on loyalty, this generation is focused on experience. What this means for potential employers, is that they must implement and adopt new sets of policies and guidelines that keep this group motivated and engaged in their work.

This group is a lot more digital savvy and is going to redefine our workplace and work culture.

International And Cross-Border Business

Economic liberalization started in China in the late 70s and the country has been growing rapidly ever since to become the 2nd biggest economy in the world. China has become the de facto manufacturing hub for the planet. On the other side, the buying power of western economies remain strong and most economies end up doing trade with these countries. And it is not just China and the developed countries. Countries like India, Brazil, South Africa, Turkey, Singapore, South Korea, and many others have joined the economic boom of liberalization of global trade. What we have seen is that there has been immense globalization that has taken place over the last 30 years.

As countries become larger economically, it is usually closely followed up by flexing political muscle power as well. Over the last few years, trade related spat between China and the US has become a constant item on the cable news network.

The COVID-19 crisis exposed one of the ugly truths about the globalized world that we live in. The world has become over-dependent on Chinese manufacturing, and in the current crisis, due to supply-chain disruption we have faced a huge barrage of issues.

As we readjust ourselves in the new normal, I believe most businesses would go back to their manufacturing base in China, but they would now, actively look to hedge their risks and certainly, explore alternate manufacturing hubs.

Not just manufacturing, free trade across the globe has meant that certain countries especially in the emerging markets have gained significantly and on the other side, it has put considerable strain on the job markets in the more developed world. Countries like India, Malaysia, Philippines, Mexico, Costa Rica, Romania, Poland, and Bulgaria have significantly benefitted from high-skilled, low cost professionals who could do the same jobs of their developed economy counterparts at a fraction of a cost.

This shift in the economic center-of-gravity that has taken place over the last 30 years, has now started showing up as discontent and unemployment issues in many countries. Political opportunists have taken full advantage of the situation and have started raising nationalistic voices across the board. This would mean that the free flow that was taking place in the recent past, would increasingly come under nationalistic scrutiny and we would be witnessing more trade barriers being put in place.

COVID-19 crisis will only accelerate this current tension, and this will create significant trade issues as we start settling into the new normal.

Deconstruction Of Jobs

I kept this point as the last trend, as you can imagine with all the changes taking place under the new normal along with the rapid changes in the technology world, this would also have a huge impact in the job market. Many of the jobs that we have known forever and have grown up with, are likely to disappear in the coming decade.

In the past, career in accounting and finance were considered lucrative and hugely sought after. The first wave of impact happened with the introduction of computers. This was followed by massive outsourcing and offshoring that started in 90s. And in the last decade, with the introduction of Robotics Process Automation (RPA), it has further eroded the value of these jobs. In the coming decade, we are likely to see more accounting and finance coordinators and managers rather than pure play bookkeepers. It is not that the need for accounting and finance has gone away, or there will not be any jobs left in this space, but the job descriptions would go through massive upheavals soon.

Similarly, in the healthcare space, artificial intelligence, big data analytics, and immersive media would mean that machines would do a lot more diagnostics and analysis in the future. And human beings would be used primarily to monitor the process instead of operating it. With VR and AR, doctors and surgeons will be able to perform their discussions and even surgeries remotely. As you can see, this would mean that technicians who can operate these new applications and manage remote collaboration would be in much more demand. And on the other hand, jobs like oncologists and other diagnostics related jobs, are going to change radically.

With cost constraints and the rise of super specialized skills soon, most companies will not be able to afford and manage these resources in-house. And from a practicality point of view, it would not even make sense if these resources are only required on a part-time basis. These conditions will give rise to gig-economy with strong job marketplace platforms supporting them. We already see this shaping up through platforms like Upwork where companies can engage crowdsourced resources for specific skills that they want, without the necessity of employment and even the whole recruitment process.

Job deconstruction is going to redefine the way we live and work. And the train has already left the station.

◆ ◆ ◆

Checklist 2: Trends Impacting Your Business

This is a checklist to get a preliminary view on how business trends in 2020s are likely to impact your business.

1. Was your organization adversely affected due to the COVID-19 crisis?

2. Do you operate in a highly competitive and limited growth market?

3. Do you have significant number of employees and other resources who work remotely?

4. What is the aging population median of your organization?

5. What is the demographic culture of your organization i.e. traditional, hierarchical, meritocratic, collaborative, etc.?

6. Does your company have a written strategy that gets shared with employees?

7. What is the relative importance given to digital initiatives in your company's strategy?

8. Do you have people from millennial and/or Gen-Z group in prominent leadership position or being groomed as high-potential?

9. Does your company conduct significant amount of cross-border business in terms of products and services?

10. Does your business use artificial intelligence, big data analytics, Blockchain, AR/VR, IoT, Smartphone based apps or immersive media solutions?

11. Does your company have experience in hiring and engaging free-lancers and consultants?

12. Does your company engage consultants at senior levels or specialized skill levels?

DIGITAL ADOPTION FRAMEWORK

Most organizations incorrectly believe that digital adoption is a binary state, either you are a digital business, or you are not. In fact, many companies buy a digital solution for a peripheral function and start proclaiming that they are a digital company.

Unfortunately, digital adoption is a full transformation. Not only does it involve enabling technologies, it also means change in operations, in leadership, in thinking, in its proliferation across different function and finally, a transformed organization.

In the past, technology would help companies to conduct activities faster, cheaper, better, and more efficient. While the same continues even today but for a blue-blooded digital organization, it means a completely transformed way of conducting business.

Based on years of experience, and conducting extensive research on various frameworks and concepts, we have created a framework that we believe will help companies to break their digital aspirations into manageable chunks. Notable models that we drew our inspiration from included Digital Capability Model[1], Business Model Canvas[2] and The Value Chain[3] to create the Digital Adoption Framework.

Digital Adoption Framework

User Experience			Digital Operations	
Digital Marketing	E-Commerce	Digital Interactions	Digital Management	Knowledge Marketing
	Market Intelligence		Digital Culture	
Data Organization			Infrastructure and Technology Management	

Figure 3.1 : Digital Adoption Framework

This framework is to create a digital adoption visualization for your organization. It has 11 functional areas where you can adopt digital and enabling technologies. This framework is a decisive canvas where you can articulate all areas where you can convert your business into a digital business and not just for only your products and services.

This aspect about digital business is essential to understand. Most of the businesses make a mistake thinking that by deploying a digital app, they can become a digital business. Whereas when you look at the canvas, you realize that there are so many different aspects that need to be considered and adopted before you can become a true digital company.

User Experience

This section covers whatever interaction you have with your customers. However, the strict definition of customers does not hold good anymore. There are people who use your products and services, there are non-customers who visit your website or comment on your social media post as well as there are those who are paying for your services and products. The entire group is now combined to new group called users. And any interaction with them on a digital platform will be covered under User eXperience or UX in short.

UX group would cover all users including your existing customers, potential buyers, enthusiasts, suppliers, alliance partners, media people or anybody who interacts with your company. By collecting data about your user's interaction, you can collect valuable insights about how your users and potential buyers are behaving and accordingly, you can tailor your marketing campaign.

In the past, companies would struggle to understand the behaviors of their potential buyers and others. Most of the available data was unstructured, and companies would have to depend on marketing research, customer surveys and independent analyst reports to gauge potential buyers. It was only when the person ended up buying your service or your product, that you started getting meaningful and structured information.

Another aspect that needs to be kept in mind is that in the digital world, it is no longer a single interaction. Thereby, experience is a collection of individual interactions that must be studied and converted to digital application.

Digital Operations

As a result of the current digital revolution, many companies would willingly and some reluctantly transform their physical companies into digital companies. In other cases, companies may diversify and create a separate and an independent business unit focusing only on digital technology.

These digital businesses will have enabling technologies as core to their operations. It can be in the form of a substantial online presence. It may have an online interface in form of a digital store for their physical goods. It may be selling wares through Facebook, Amazon, or other E-commerce platform. It may be using big-data analytics to generate insights. It can be artificial intelligence being used for diagnostics. Or it could use Blockchain as a multi-party consortium. In other words, there are diverse set of manifestations that a digital company may have. The critical element is to have an enabling technology as core to the business.

The first kind of digital operations would be those that are completely online businesses. Yellow pages setup their online platform in 2006 but it was only in January 2019 that they completely moved to the online world.

The second kind of businesses are those who have physical products or provide services in the physical world but their business sourcing and selling takes place through an E-commerce platform. It can be fashion brands, books, devices, gadget, and various other items. The key differentiator is that the business solely relies on selling through E-commerce platform. There is a burgeoning set of businesses that are thriving on selling products through Amazon, Bol.com, Zalando and other online platforms. Many of these businesses are broker businesses, and we now see an increase in the number of businesses that solely manufacture for E-commerce platforms.

The third kind of businesses are those which are using enabling technologies like big-data analytics, AI, IoT, Blockchain and VR/AR as their core. These businesses will be digitally native almost from the start. Healthcare diagnostics companies, market research firms, and even some service providers who will use digital technology as a core, will fall in this category.

Certain aspects of this section may have an overlap with other elements but keep in mind, that this section is relevant when a business has completely transformed itself into a digital business and shuts their previous business, or they have created an independent business unit to be digital.

Digital Marketing

Getting structured data systematically in the physical world, marketing campaigns have always been a challenge. However, as our interactions have increased in the digital world, so has the amount of digital footprint that we leave. These digital footprints provide rich information about your buyers as well as potential consumers. The data generated from these interactions can be systematically collected and analyzed for insights by companies.

One of the significant developments that has taken place in this space, is the introduction of digital marketing funnel. Some of you may be familiar with "AIDA" model in marketing. Though this model has existed for more than a hundred years, but with digital marketing AIDA model has shot into prominence.

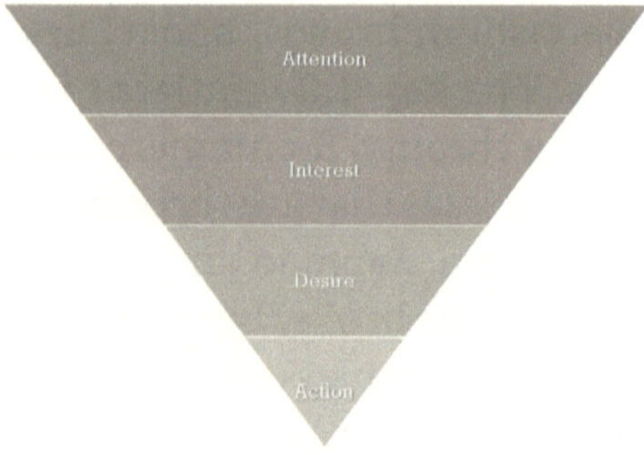

Figure 3.2: AIDA Digital Marketing Funnel

AIDA stands for Attention, Interest, Desire and Action. With so much of interaction taking place in the digital space, companies can design and develop specific components for each stage. The aim of the AIDA model is to take a potential customer through the complete experience journey starting from the awareness stage till the actual purchase.

Attention

Once a strategic campaign has been decided and signed off by the leadership, this is where the digital marketing funnel starts. In this stage, you would ask the following questions:
- Who is your target group or groups? *User profiling*
- What are some of the problems and challenges faced by

your target group? *Empathy mapping*

- What kind of solutions is your target group looking for? *Market intelligence*

- How can your solution potentially help your target group? *Product-market fit*

In addition, you need to conduct research on the following:

- How is the target group articulating their challenges and pains? Social media chatter, industry report, 3rd party surveys, sales team's feedback, etc.

- How are they expecting to find a solution? Are they contacting consultants, attending seminars on this topic, surfing specific websites?

- How are you planning to create awareness and seek their attention? What channels would you use? What messaging and copyrighting will you need to do?

Depending on the answers to the above questions, you will design your marketing campaign. Depending on the channel, you will start creating content for the same. Obviously, different channels would mean different approaches. An Instagram may need a visual story, a twitter would need punch one-liners or product offers, and your email will need a grabbing headline.

Interest

Once you have created an attention in the market, and you find that your target group is showing interest, you must figure out how to maintain that interest.

And how do you figure out that your initial awareness campaign has generated an interest? Through clicks, time-spent, opens, etc.

For them to maintain their interest, your company shares some in-depth blogs, articles or throws in initial hooks in the form of offering them some freebies if they continue to be a part of your target group's journey.

Desire

Some businesses can not differentiate between these 2 steps: interest and desire. Interest is where your target group is curious to learn more about your products or your services. Desire is where your target group is convinced about your product and services being a potential solution for your problems. They are now evaluating other aspects including affordability, validation, market feedback, any negative reviews as well as repeat inspection.

Increase in the number of opens of the same emails, increased visit frequency to your website, potential interaction with your chatbots and maybe customer service all signifies an increase in the desirability of your target group.

Action

This is the last stage of the funnel where your target group buys your product or your services. You must be careful about putting noticeably clear Call-to-Actions (CTAs) at this stage so that your potential buyer can smoothly transition from being a prospect to an actual buyer.

There is a delicate approach required for this stage. You need to position your CTAs very strategically on your webpage or other medium. You do not want to appear over-zealous and on the other side, you do not want to lose your potential buyer since the person could not find the CTA button.

With digital marketing campaign, you now have an opportunity to guide your target group in a structured way to buy your products and services. And this structured approach can hugely increase your conversion rate as well as your revenue line.

E-Commerce

For many companies that deal with physical products, digital technologies can offer them virtual marketplaces that they can use to sell their products. This is however, not restricted to physical products only. You can use platforms like Udemy, Coursera and others to sell your digital training products. You can sell your own eBooks on Amazon or Nooks. You can even use affiliate marketing technics to sell your products on a 3rd party platform.

These virtual marketplaces primarily come in two flavors. The first flavor is where you use your own platform. You can sell your trainings, diagnostics, eBooks, software, application, cloud-solutions on your own platform or platforms that give you dedicated cloud space. Platforms like Thinkific or Teachable would provide platforms where you can sell your online training. The cloud space and web pages are dedicated to your business only. Whether you have a single product or a complete portfolio, you have a dedicated web link. This is highly suitable for businesses that have a range of products in their portfolio, and it is good for your brand building. Essentially, these platforms are giving you enabling tools to fast track your digital adoption. Both Thinkific and Teachable provide pre-defined templates to create online courses so make it dramatically easy for businesses to create a professional looking online training platform.

The second flavor is 3rd party platforms like Amazon, eBay, Airbnb, Upwork when the actual digital marketplace is owned by a 3rd party. This is suitable for businesses that want a digital platform for their physical products. It can be fashion, retail, books, or even spare capacity in your house, or you want to solicit freelance work for your specialist skills, these e-commerce platforms have come a long way. Platforms like Amazon and eBay are multi-product platforms where you can sell your gadgets, but you can sell books as well. This can be attractive for broker businesses who can source products from physical markets and sell them through these platforms. Platforms like Airbnb and Upwork are specialized marketplaces. Airbnb would sell spare capacity rooms for short-term rental whereas Upwork is a digital marketplace for skills.

Depending on the nature of your business and the kind of market access you are looking for you can decide what is more relevant for your business. Moreover, it is not an either-or choice. Many businesses choose both the options. As a publisher, you may decide to sell your books through multiple channels. A fashion brand may have their own channels, but they can also, sell through 3rd party channels. In fact, most of the fashion houses choose both the options.

At the end, if you can get benefitted from being on multiple platforms, then that is the approach you need to take. However, if it dilutes your brand value, you may decide to stay with your own platform.

Market Intelligence

There are huge amounts of data that is available in the public domains. This is the element where you use specialized skills to gather data both structured and unstructured from the market, from third-party databases, research journals, educational institutes, and feedback from your customers, suppliers, and partners. You harness the data to extract useful information and knowledge that can be leveraged to create a competitive edge for you.

There are multiple ways this available data can be used. Here are five uses under this category that I believe you will find useful.

Potential clients

By scouring through large swathes of data, you can get a deep understanding about the market. You can obtain powerful insights through UX research and digital marketing. This can be a great source of potential clients for you.

Competitive edge

By studying and distilling information from public domains,

you get a far better comprehension about your market. How are your competitors faring, what are the new trends in the market, what are some of the potential challenges, who is disrupting your market and most importantly, what products are performing well and at what price points, are just a few strategic questions that can get addressed by market intelligence. You can recreate your customer segmentation, create specific pricing and discounts by segments, as well as look at product diversification by understanding the dynamics of the market.

Whitepaper

By analyzing data, you can create your own market intelligence. This market intelligence can then be used to create whitepaper, blogs, and other insights that you can share online. This can be used as a lead-magnet for your business

Research-as-a-service

Companies that have a strong base in a certain industry and have access to a team of analysts, can easily create research-as-a-service as a potential product. While there are huge amounts of information available on the world wide web, most of it is unstructured and there is a genuine paucity of quality insights. Having a strong base in a certain industry, can give you an edge to create value-added research-as-a-service for your business.

Partnerships, alliances, and M&A

By understanding the market dynamics, you will also, recognize the players that operate in your existing market as well as new one. You can use this information to identify potential partners and alliances to access new markets or consolidate your position in the existing market. You can even explore possibilities of creating joint-ventures and in some, cases pursue an acquisition or investment strategy as well. This form of market intelligence is extensively used by strategic business buyers, private equities, and institutional investors.

Overall, market intelligence as a category had limited power prior to the internet revolution. And now, it can be a formidable tool for any business irrespective of their size or location.

Digital Interactions

This element covers all the channels, platforms and media being used to interact with your users, potential buyers, and customers. Some users use a single medium to interact with a business, others use several channels, and in some cases, an average user interchangeably uses different channels at different points in time.

In the past you only had a limited number of ways that you could interact. You could use land mail, fax, email, phone calls and physical meetings. But now in the digital medium there are hundreds of different options and channels that you can choose from.

You can use MailChimp to send out emails to your subscribers, you may use YouTube to share videos, you may use LinkedIn for professional digital advertisements, you may use simple emails for business transactions, you may leave comments on the website and various other methods.

To keep a track of different channels and their effectiveness, you need understand the dynamics of each of these channels. This will not only allow you to connect with your users through different mediums but will also tell you which channels are more effective in comparison to others. An example that I can share from our own experience is when we advertise with LinkedIn versus Facebook. With LinkedIn, we tend to get more professional interactions whereas Facebook provides the fun element.

We have divided these interactions in the following categories:

Social media

It includes platforms like Facebook, Instagram, LinkedIn, Twitter, and the others. Your users interact with your company pages on these platforms, or follow key people of your leadership team, or the same could be on your events page or a showcase page.

Usually, users will use these platforms to provide feedback or voice opinions. In some cases, they will complain about your product or services. In other cases, they might post positive comments about you.

Most importantly, through social media you can create a fan-base, a community of users who like your company as well as a collaboration channel between you and your users.

Moreover, from the interactions you have, you will be able to gauge the levels of interest of your users in your posts based on likes, shares, and comments

Content platforms

Content platforms like YouTube, Podcasts, SlideShare and blog sites let you post audios, videos and blogs related to your business, your products, and services. You can post informational material, opinions, market intelligence as well as promotional material on these platforms. These platforms can provide great avenues to share your experience, knowledge, and expertise with rest of the world.

E-Commerce platforms

This sub-category covers platforms like Amazon, and others that you use to display, share, and/or sell your products. This is a platform where users leave comments, providing you with a great source of feedback about your products and services.

Web traffic

Traffic that flows to your website in another form of inter-action with your users. From the volume, you can discern the condition of your website. By studying their behavior while interacting with your website can give you profound insights. You can easily figure out; what pages attract your users and what do not. The most important thing is that Google has its algorithm based on user interaction with your platform, for ranking your page during a search process

Email

You now have the option of keeping in touch with your users through individual emails sent from your own mailbox or it can be through mass broadcasts and newsletters sent through a 3rd-party like Mailchimp and Mailer lite. If your business has hundreds of users, it may be difficult to keep sending them individually crafted emails. There is a time and place where you will need to send those ones as well. However, when you need to send bulk emails, platforms like Mailchimp make a huge difference. You can analyze how many emails were opened, how many people clicked on links in your email, how many people shared your email, etc. At the same time, if people are no longer interested, they can also choose to unsubscribe to your email broadcasts. This can be a cumbersome process if you had to update the status of these users manually in your CRM or lead database. However, with in-built functionalities, these platforms get these administrations done automatically.

Survey platforms

Survey platforms like SurveyMonkey and Typeforms are great

tools to collect information from your users and independent people about your business, product, as well as market research information. Many businesses regularly keep in touch with engaging their users through surveys and focus groups especially before they launch a new product or a new campaign.

Many businesses overlook the power of using surveys to interact with their customers and users in a non-intrusive way.

Businesses may choose one medium versus the other, or a combination but they should remember that it is no longer sufficient to treat each of these channels independently but they should be treated as part of a cohesive, coordinated set. When you run a campaign now, you need to run it as a single campaign with an omni-channel perspective. An average user toggles between different channels during the same campaign. A user may read your email from their smartphones which was sent from MailChimp, reply to the email that goes to your own mailbox, download the freebie from their desktop and then share the news about the freebie on Facebook.

Another important aspect of an omni-channel is to ensure that the campaign is seen by your target group. With so much of information being shared, and so many emails ending up in junk folders, it is quite possible that the emails are either missed out, not seen or not actioned upon by your users before they move on to the next item. That is why, it is important that other channels can re-enforce the visibility of your campaigns.

Digital Management

To run an organization, you need a full-fledged management system and leadership team. Similarly, to run a digital program or a digital business, you need a similar construct. You will need Digital savvy leadership, specialized skills, change management as well as governance mechanisms, performance measurements, project management office and various other components including policies and guidelines to make it an effective digital organization.

Digital savvy leadership

Many businesses that struggle with digital adoption is primarily due to their executive leadership team's lack of understanding of the power of these enabling technologies. On the other side, companies that have digitally savvy CEO or COO have been extremely successful in making that transition. CXOs who understand the power of social interactions through online platforms or understand how market intelligence can be effectively used to gather strong insights are likely to develop better understanding about their users and consumers. Similarly, executives who understand the power of AI or are using IoT in their business, can creatively develop a portfolio of products.

Digitally savvy does not mean that they need to know how to write codes in these platforms. It means that they have a good understanding of how these enabling technologies can be effectively adopted for their businesses and how they can help their organizations grow.

Specialized skills

Adoption of digital technologies does not mean you need to hire dozens of data scientists or AI engineers. It means that you need a work force that is adept in working with digital marketing funnels, social media, content marketing and several other aspects. In some cases, you may need to hire super specialists and quants, but it is also possible that you may acquire these services from a 3rd party on a pay-as-you-go service or partner with them for digital co-creation.

Change management

As your organization transforms into a digital organization, you need to focus on the requirements of change management. This can mean communication at different points of transition, but this can also mean counselling through the job deconstruction process

Governance

Your digital organization will need its own governance mechanism, management as well as clearly defined performance measurements. This will help you achieve your digital adoption objectives easily but also, provide you with the mechanism to manage daily operations.

Policies and procedures

Many of your organizational policies and procedures will no longer be valid or be relevant once your digital adoption process is completed. Your company will need to revamp your policies and procedures. This could be related to the usage of digital media, online presence but also, restrictions and information security related to your company information.

Digital Culture

To ensure that your organization gets truly digital, you will need to ensure that your organization culture also reflects that. Without the necessary thinking, openness, eagerness to learn and continuously improve, your organization will always have a chance of going back to old ways of doing things. No matter how exciting the digital technologies may sound, habits have a way of creeping back into our lives if we do not address them properly.

Rapid Innovation

First and foremost, required for a digital organization is to have rapid innovation. This is to ensure that there is no procrastination happening once a round of innovations are conducted. Secondly, it creates a buzz amongst the teams that ensures further engagement, motivation and most important, brings new ideas that can create business growth.

Fail fast, learn faster

Rapid innovation would also, mean that many experiments would fail. Instead of getting into a blame game, a digital organization should have guidelines and frameworks in place that foster quick analysis and learning from the experiment so that those faults can be avoided in further experiments.

Experiment in volume

One can truly extract good insights when experiments are conducted in volume. They will ensure deeper understanding of the market and user behavior. It will also prevent from getting any parallax views which may result in distorted understanding.

Enabling tools

To conduct experiments and innovation, teams need to be given right tools, templates, software. With the plethora of open and free software, companies have a lot of options to choose from. However, for consistency and standardization, care must be taken, and consensus driven in the organization on what preferred tools and software to use. If you plan to use a tool, use Eventbrite as a tool to attract people but use Mailchimp as your CRM. Also, do not have some of your team members storing information in Eventbrite and the others in Mailchimp to avoid confusion.

Training

New digital platforms as well as software tools would need adequate training for the workforce. In addition, there need to be regular refreshers for the team to keep them updated. Apart from that, teams also need to ensure entire organizations get trained in new applications.

Mentoring

During the transformation stage and the new digital organization, there will be a constant need for supervising, coaching, and mentoring the larger teams. You will need to think of change agents, champions and group coaches who can help, support and mentor organizations in digital adoption.

Digital culture is an important foundational element to create a sustainable organization. The change in culture needs to be driven with the right ingredients and elements.

Knowledge Management

Every organization sits on top of a mountain of unearthed value. Most of them do not realize the importance or do not have the capability of unlocking the potential from this mountain of value.

The extraction and distribution of these experiential values to drive growth and effectiveness of an organization is termed as knowledge management. To use these bites of knowledge in marketing would be referred to as knowledge marketing.

While knowledge management is important for all businesses, it can be of immense value for human centric or knowledge centric organizations.

In the digital era that we live in, it is no longer enough to just talk about features of your products and services. In fact, due to digital access many businesses are struggling to maintain their differentiator. Let us look at consulting business. No matter what your services are, there will be hundreds if not thousands who will appear to give the same services, bring the same benefits and saying the same thing about their services.

On the other hand, the businesses who share their tools, technics, templates, case studies and experiences through white-papers, blogs, videos, and other channels get better quality leads and higher conversion rate.

Knowledge marketing becomes a key differentiating tool for any digital business. The reasons are described below.

Credibility

The moment you create a whitepaper, publish a blog, and put a video online, it establishes you as an instant authority of your subject. People believe that if you have put something in the public domain then you must be credible.

Relevance

Many businesses may struggle to adopt any change. This problem gets compounded when the technology landscape is rapidly changing around them. Businesses may understand the power of an enabling technology but if they cannot create relevance, they cannot conceptualize a solution for their own business. I remember a conversation a few years back. I was speaking with an executive leader of a large multinational corporation on the benefits of Blockchain. While the person understood the functionalities of Blockchain, he was struggling to conceptualize on how to apply it to his organization. I had to help him walk through a couple of scenarios before he clearly understood the relevance and thus the benefit of the technology.

Many people would study and understand the functionalities of new technologies but without comprehension on how to apply it, they would stay on the fence.

Pull marketing

Best part of knowledge marketing is that it is a pull-marketing. As you establish credibility and relevance of digital technology, you will find that potential clients come to you more than your need to go to them. The credibility also, reduces the need for extensive convincing that is usually required through other means. Moreover, it gives you an edge to charge premium pricing for your services.

Fear of IP

Many companies are afraid of adopting knowledge marketing. Quite commonly I hear this argument from companies, that if they share their experience, their IP will become public and maybe adopted by their competitors.

"KEEPING KNOWLEDGE ERODES POWER. SHARING IS THE FUEL TO YOUR GROWTH ENGINE." - UNKNOWN

There are five things I would like to say in support of this:
-    One is that if it were so easy then every business would become super profitable businesses by reading books.
-    Second, your experience and expertise can never be taken away from you. It also, never reduces. It only grows.
-    By not letting your experience being shared, you are only restricting your business from growing.
-    If you have thought about it, there must be hundred others who have thought about it as well. So, you are not unique and you, are not the only one that can solve the problem
-    There is always a place to protect your IP (like a secret sauce). But it should not be confused experience.
By effectively marketing your knowledge, you can create a robust knowledge management organization. Knowledge market-

ing can tremendously increase your visibility in the market, lend massive credibility and the best part is that customers come to you rather than you chase them and pay a premium fee.

Data Organization

The era prior to digital adoption, we would talk about supply-chain, logistics, manufacturing, assembly-lines, and operations. With digital adoption and gargantuan amounts of data being generated, we would see similar structures being positioned to manage data. This new setup is going to be called data organization.

Data organization will be at the confluence of digital technology and conventional management structures. Governance, strategy, performance measurement, information flow, data economics as well as data sovereignty will need to be revamped.

Data ownership

One of the biggest questions soon, will be around ownership of data. With increased awareness around data privacy and regulations being implemented, organizations need to review what data can be owned by them vs not.

Every time I get a call from my bank, my bank asks me about my date of birth as well as specific items like my home address. What if I do not feel comfortable with sharing this information with a 3rd party like a bank.

If we look at another example, your impression would be quite different. Suppose you had a pain in your abdomen, and you had to visit a doctor. The doctor would ask you a few questions and make a diagnostic assessment. This is where it gets interesting. As the pain was yours, is it your data to own? What would be able to do with the data without the intervention of a doctor. Is doctor the owner of the diagnostic result data?

Data is the new gold. Questions like the ones above will be asked more often. In the future, these voices will only get pronounced and amplified.

Digital assembly line

Like in the physical world, raw material goes through an assembly line before it converts into a finished product. Similarly, in digital organizations, flow of data will also follow a similar path. And as with the physical structure, digital structure will also have different teams with different value-creation, deliverables, and accountability.

Digital waste

Huge amounts of data are being generated every second. With further advances in technology, the data management problem is only going to get bigger. And one of the big issues is going to be around digital waste.

Most organizations will not pay heed to this as digital storage devices get cheaper. However, the problem is likely to arise in the form of disposal, archival and retrieval.

Look at the care that you take disposing physical letters. How many of us, can say the same thing about your e-mails? Millions of documents get created before we can bat an eyelid. You may have taken measures to protect your data on your desktop. But how about all the social media posts, all the documents that you have shared in the cyber-space and all the transactions that you were involved in, but are not actively aware? Information about you that is stored by your bank, by your credit card provider, by the loyalty program cards and many other places. As you know only too well, many cyberattacks take place randomly, and companies lose valuable customer information.

Data organization is no longer a nice to have, it is time that organizations start reviewing this seriously.

Infrastructure Management

This is the element of DAF. To support everything that is required from a technology perspective to make your company digital is covered under this element. What applications to use, what sort of storage facilities, cloud computing, software licenses and hardware required to run a digital organization, are all included in this element.

Scaling flexibility

In a digital business, there is a going to be an increased need of flexibility in scaling up and scaling down as per the need of the organization. When a new system gets implemented, organizations may need to scale-up their environments to cater for testing and development. During a stable operations period, this requirement becomes redundant.

Now, with Google, Microsoft, and Amazon, all trying to woo customers to get to their platform, interoperability will need to be reviewed carefully as well.

Cyber and information security

Much of the information that is in the public cloud has a lot of security and protection these days. However, the challenge is with millions of freebie apps that are being used, it is the unstructured data that is constantly being downloaded to your devices and suspicious website visits that make your system more prone to cyberattacks.

A sinister side of information security is going to be doctored data and fake news. With information being shared so openly, in such quick time especially in case of sensational news, organizations will be faced with double problems. One is the information security itself and the other one, will be damage control.

Infrastructure organization

Infrastructure management in the digital world needs to be thought through again. In the past, organizations needed to maintain specialized skills within their own organizations, to manage expensive hardware and software. Now, with much of physical infrastructure being replaced by cloud-computing, we will need different kinds of skills in our organization. Rather than maintaining specialized skills, we will need people who are good at problem solving and collaborating with other people include remote teams as well as support teams of the service provider.

In the future, business continuity and disaster recovery plans, will get replaced with digital twins' model. This again, would need different skills than the past.

Finally, any specialized software and tools like IoT, AI, robotics, and managing digital funnels will all need a new set of skills.

Organizations will need to think of reskilling their own staff as well as get used to the idea of gig economy, where it hires people on short-term contracts or even part time rather than full-time employees.

Summary

These were the 11 items that make the Digital Adoption Framework (DAF). DAF is meant to provide a structure by which a company can convert its organizational digital adoption strategy to specific operational level visualization.

By discussing this framework with your team, you should be able to generate a huge number of ideas from which you should easily be able to short-list and prioritize the ideas that you can further develop.

Using this framework, you can start building your story and create a detailed strategy based on solid foundational blocks. With the framework, you should be confidently able to embark on a digital adoption journey.

Whether you are going to completely become a digital business, a physical business with a digital front-end or simply adopt few digital elements will depend on the individual needs of your organization. As mentioned earlier, whether we like it or not, like in the 90s where most companies moved their information to servers and computers, similarly, in this digital age, all companies irrespective of what business they are in, will move to become technology companies.

◆ ◆ ◆

Checklist 3: Baselining For Digital Adoption

This is a checklist that you should use before you start using DAF.

1. What is the compelling reason that is driving your organization to become digital?

2. Do you have digital expertise in your executive and senior management team?

3. Is there a separate digital strategy of your organization?

4. Has your organization run transformational projects in the last 5-7 years like ERP implementation, or any other project that impacted the entire organization and which needed significant involvement of people in various parts of the organization?

5. How would you describe your business's social media presence? What is the primary use of the social media presence?

6. Does your organization run digital marketing campaigns?

7. What are the different digital channels that your company uses to interact with its customers?

8. How does your company create awareness about your products, services, capabilities and experience with non-customers, and other users?

9. Does your company publish white-papers, articles, blogs,

and videos consistently, or is it ad hoc in nature?

10. Do you have a digital team led by a chief digital officer or is it handled by your IT team?

11. Is your organization using any of the latest enabling technologies in main functions (not peripheral) including IoT, AI, Big data analytics, Blockchain and/or VR/AR?

12. What 11 elements is your company likely to adopt?

13. Which of the 11 elements is your company likely to avoid and why?

14. Is your organization experienced in engaging highly skilled and expensive external resources?

15. In your opinion, if your organization did not adopt digital technology in the next 5 years, what do you foresee is going to be the future of your company?

16. Do you think your current job will exist in 5 years time?

◆ ◆ ◆

Notes:

1. Jace An, 77 Building Blocks of Digital Transformation, written by a digital practitioner, Story Tree FDC, 2019

2. Alexander Osterwalder and Yves Pigneur, Business Model Generation: A Handbook for Visionaries, Game Changers, and Challengers, John Wiley & Sons, Inc., 2010

3. Michael E. Porter, Competitive Advantage: Creating and Sustaining Superior Performance, Free Press, 1985

DIGITAL STRATEGY

To help with the strategy, we have explored several tools and frameworks so far. As digital adoption has a strong-linkage with product-market fit, Ansoff's matrix fitted nicely to our requirement. We have adapted the model with digital products for businesses to create a digital strategy.

Ansoff Matrix

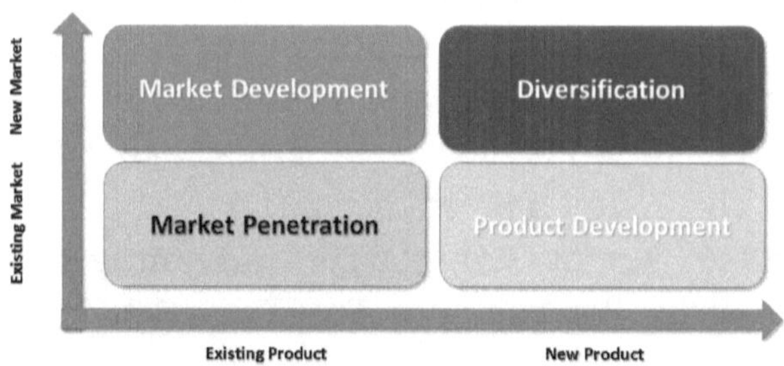

Figure 4.1: Original Ansoff Growth Matrix

Igor Ansoff had written a paper in 1957, here he shared a product-market quadrant on how to strategically approach business growth. The original quadrant had four blocks:
- Existing product in existing market: Market penetration
- Existing product in new market: Market development

- New product in existing market: Product development
- New product in new market: Diversification

We find that this matrix is highly appropriate even for digital products as well. That is why, we have reframed Ansoff matrix for Digital Strategy.

Digital Strategy: Redefined Ansoff Matrix

New Market | Existing Market

| Market Development | Globalization |
| Organic Growth | Digital Diversification |

Existing Product | Digital Product

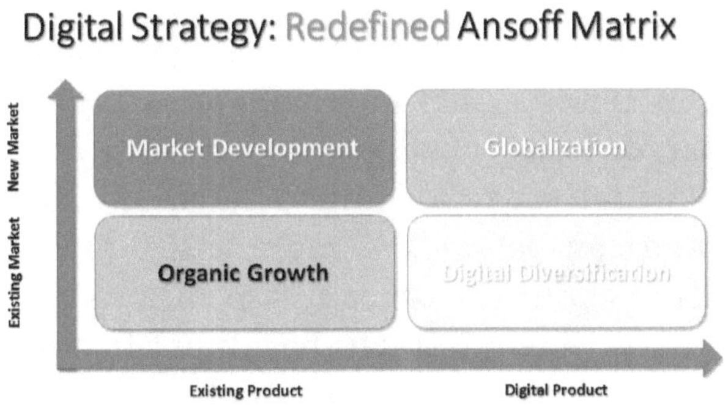

Figure 4.2: Redefined Ansoff Matrix for Digital Strategy

If you see carefully, you will see that the left column primarily refers to existing products. We can continue to use these blocks but add digital processes to support the existing products and services. And the right column is dependent on you creating new digital products or services as part of your strategy.

Digital Strategy With Non-Digital Products

Existing Product and Existing Market

This category refers to current products or services being sold in your existing market, also referred to as organic growth. In this category, companies look for internal efficiencies and new methods of marketing their products in existing markets.

Under this category, we will explore how enabling technologies can be used to boost your growth. As mentioned in the prior chapters, it can be challenging to grow if the market conditions are not very conducive but with digital technology you can disrupt the conditions and extract exceptional growth for your company.

Most of the strategy focuses around either driving efficiency or gaining market advantage, or both.

Efficiency of operations

<u>Operational efficiency</u>: Under this category we explore technology infused changes that can make existing operations go faster, cheaper, or better. These would include migrating most of your user experience to a digital medium so that it generates data and can be tracked more easily. It will help collect information about the users and in turn optimize internal processes to manage requirement fulfilment in a more efficient way. Optimizing infrastructure through cloud-computing or SaaS would be another option that can be leveraged by organizations. Bringing all the digital and social media interactions under one umbrella, streamlining, and aligning them under a common approach through digital interactions can significantly improve operations. Businesses no longer must rely on conventional marketing through physical interactions, and depend on IT for technology support, communications team for content and sales, for daily interactions with your customers and prospects.

<u>Management efficiency</u>: This category refers to innovative and structured ways to improve effectiveness of the management. These would include improving operating rigors, management governance and performance management, key metrics and indicators through digital means, You can use LEAN management's piece flow framework and use it to create a Data organization by replacing the physical part with digital data. With the right level of digital management and digital culture, you can bring about significant efficiency specially in terms of increased accountability and innovative experiments.

<u>Financial efficiency</u>: This category deals with investments, cash-flow management, income, revenue, margins and most im-

portantly, accounting. Organizations may go through financial restructuring, debt-financing, experiment with cash cycles, and finance capital investments to improve the financial health of an organization. With digital elements plugged in, you can consolidate real-time data and create reports that can help strategic decision making. With big data analysis and artificial intelligence, you can also create dynamic pricing that can boost performance.

Market competitiveness

In this strategy approach, companies look at their commercial and revenue generating engines for ways to improve their top-line.

<u>Sales transformation</u>: Under this category, sales processes can be radically changed by adoption of digital apps and enabling technologies. An average salesperson spends about 60-70% of their time on administrative activities including preparing reports, filling forms, internal meetings, management meetings and others. Using RPAs (Robotics Process Automation), admin apps on mobile devices and other web-based workflows and document control processes, you can easily create a more efficient environment. By doing this, even if you can reduce the time spent from 70% to less than 50%, your salesperson would have 20% more time that they can spend in front of their customers. On top, adding UX research and customer intimacy can drive production of rich data that can be beneficial in your sales process.

<u>Marketing transformation</u>: This segment includes digitally repurposing awareness campaigns, managing multi-channel marketing and lead generation. Using digital marketing funnel, can provide a deep understanding of consumers and the market. With AIDA (Attention, Interest, Desire, Action) model, you can strive towards a better sales conversion rate. By using email marketing, knowledge marketing and social media interactions, you can bolster your brand and create better lead magnets for your organization.

<u>Portfolio variation</u>: You may improve or modify some aspects of your services or your product by including a digital byproduct or a service to expand upon your portfolio. If you are a training or a consulting company, you can add digital interactions, videos, and material on online platforms. You can add market intelligence report to support your physical products or services.

<u>Customer experience</u>: this is one category that is increasingly becoming vital for organizations specially in B2C businesses. By initiating good measures, if you can improve the customer experience and your customer acknowledge then you have a far better chance of getting more business. The reverse is true as well, but the impact tends to be much greater in case of a negative experience. What can you do to enrich your customer experience when they use your products and services?

Existing Product in New Market

This category refers to expansion to new markets with your existing product. When a business plans to expand into a new market, there will be a significant amount of market intelligence that needs to be gathered, brand building needs to be done, and one has to pursue business development efforts and in some cases, look for a potential local partner to access the market.

Chances are that there is little to no brand awareness in the new market. This of course, is true for most businesses unless you have an iconic brand like Virgin, Coca Cola, Toyota, and the likes of those. Even for these marquee brands some work still needs to be done for local awareness. But for most brands, it needs to start from scratch.

New markets may have certain nuances and have specific requirements. Local language is one of them. Cultural and geographic sensibilities need to be taken into consideration. Localization is another requirement. This can be manifested in various forms ranging from locally sourcing products, local alliances to having a certain percentage of locals in your workforce.

Growing businesses in a new market has different sets of challenges compared to your existing market. You often need to reset your thinking for a new market. With incomplete thinking, more companies perish than succeed in the new market.

<u>Business development</u>: To create visibility, you need to actively market your company and start building your brand. This would include reaching out to potential customers, but it would also, mean reaching out to your contacts, well-wishers and other experts who can provide great insights, and share technics about how to penetrate the market. Social interaction is a key part of this category. By using digital marketing, UX research as well as market intelligence, you can increase the chances of entering a new market successfully.

<u>Alliances/Partners</u>: if it is a new country or a new geography you may want to look for local partners and alliances to promote your product. Local partners and alliances can add a lot of value to your business. Their understanding of the market, their connections with potential customers as well as their awareness of prevailing business and government practices make your local partners valuable. Market intelligence again, can provide a good understanding of the market dynamics as well as highlight the players that operate in the market.

<u>Product Customization</u>: Some of the products or services may require localization in terms of language, regulatory requirements, customs, and existing practices. Getting a Halal certification for meat products, or a CE certification for electronic goods, labeling in different languages are just a few examples. Market intelligence, digital interactions and UX research can help you tremendously. Using digital interactions, you can also start creating initial traction with the market even before your product is available in the market.

<u>Brand Awareness</u>: When you enter a new market, you need to spend time and effort creating an awareness on your brand, product, and services. This can be through paid advertisements, digital marketing campaigns but also, seminars, talk shows and events, as well as a multi-channel digital interactions.

Strategy With Digital Products

When it comes to digital adoption approach, one must keep in mind that in most cases, digital strategic approach is not just about making processes run faster, better, cheaper and more efficiently but you can also, explore if you can create digital products that can be sold in either existing markets or even better, launched globally.

Digital adoption with digital products should be a new product introduction either in the existing markets, new markets, or both. It is not an efficiency game but an operational approach to the market.

Let us look at the right side of the page where we have the replaced the "new products" in the original Ansoff Growth Matrix with "digital product"

We made this tweak because a new product in the usual sense of it tends to have similar characteristics like the original product. Digital products on the other hand, have very distinct and different features that are significantly different in their market dynamics. Scalability, cheap implementation, quick pivot, democratization, fast go-to-market are just a few features that put them in a vastly different category in terms of business dynamics.

Digital Product in Existing market

We will refer to launching digital products in existing markets, as digital diversification.

As the digital product features are vastly different from your existing product, you will have to think of it not just as an introduction of a new product in the existing market but new strategy. Your digital product will need vastly different levels of support, marketing and sales, and a new business model compared to your existing product and thus, we call it digital business diversification. Thinking digital operations, data organization, digital management, digital culture, and infrastructure management will play a key role under this category.

Digital Product in New market

As digital products can be ported easily over the internet across the globe and with the right content and structure can be made available to a large number of people at the same time, new market in the digital world should be seen as a "global" market. The moment you put something online, it can potentially be accessed by people across the globe whether you like or not. Unless you have interfaced with a user login page and decided to launch your product in Esperanto language, your digital product will be visible to all the digital community irrespective of the geography that you operate in.

That is why, it is important that when you think of extending your product to a new market, you should be considering a global strategy instead. However, you need to keep in mind that digital applications can give you much wider market access, but each market has its own nuances that must be considered. They can be in terms of restrictions, regulations, taxation, adaptability, or simply personal bias. That is why, it is important to approach globalization with proper diligence and market responsibility.

Another critical challenge with going global with a digital product is that the allure of millions of customers online can be strong. But just because they are there, does not mean they will buy from you. There are also thousands of sellers like you in the online world. Exercise caution, before you go spending huge amounts on digital customer acquisition approaches.

Most important point is however, that if you can create a robust globalization plan with a good digital product or a service, sky is the limit for your company's growth.

Combining the features of digital technology and with a sound business strategy, you are ready to embark on an exceptional growth journey. This is repurposed Ansoff Growth Matrix for Digital Strategy.

Closing remark

There are plenty of ways that you can grow your company with digital adoption. Before I end the chapter, there are a few tips that I would like to share.

First, every company is different and will need customized approach. However, most of the underlying fundamental elements are the same. These are the ones that we have included in DAF. You need to see the suitability and relevance for your business.

Secondly, creating a strategy with a single element of DAF is not going to cut it for your organization. You need to select a good few to create an effective strategy that will give you an exceptional growth.

Last, digital strategy is not a good to have but a necessity as we sit at the cusp of the start of a new digitally defining decade.

Checklist 4: Preparing For Digital Strategy

1. What potential product or service of your company can be converted into digital product?

2. Are there any digital competitors for your business?

3. What type of digital products and services are used in your market and industry?

4. How digitally savvy are your customers in professional as well as personal spheres?

5. How wide is the usage of social media in your industry?

6. How often do you connect with your customers through email and another digital medium?

7. Which of the functions should you consider in-scope for digital transformation?

8. What will be the potential loss of impact for out-of-scope digital elements?

9. What size of market in terms of geography are you likely to pursue for digital expansion?

10.   What sort of leadership involvement would you need to create an effective program?

11.   What sort of digital marketing are you likely to pursue?

12.   How can you leverage the expertise and experience in your organization to create content for knowledge marketing?

13.   What sort of expertise do you expect to be required to pursue a digital strategy?

INNOVATIVE DIGITAL ACCELERATORS

I n this section, I am going to share eight digital accelerators that can give exponential growth for your company. Based on experience, interaction with hundreds of industry expert and research, we have created this curated list of eight accelerators.

Digitalization Of Products

In this accelerator, you produce a digital version of your product. You can also include part of the order fulfilment, installation or service delivery that can be converted into a digital product.

As mentioned in the previous chapters, cost of production of digital products are usually cheap, can be scaled easily and deployed quickly. Imagine, with similar resources as conventional, you now have the ability of creating thousands of digital replicas without a fuss. This can give you a huge lift in a noticeably short period of time. Low capital outlay at the initial stages and relatively low maintenance makes this preferred accelerator of choice for many companies.

And of course, one should not forget that in many cases, being online, will give you unprecedented access to wider and even global markets.

Retail stores, supermarkets, fashion brands and other productized items can adopt e-commerce platforms to get access to bigger set of potential consumers. Whether you develop your own, or use a third-party platform like Amazon, E-bay, Zalando, Bol.com and others, to showcase your products, you choose the platforms that work best for you. Many companies choose to go with both the options, to have their own platform and to sell on 3rd party e-commerce platforms.

Even cafes, restaurants and other eateries can increase their sales through 3rd party digital delivery platforms like UberEATS, Food Panda and Deliveroo. Some people may argue that these 3rd party platforms charge an enormous premium for their services. The reality is this premium is on the additional business that you never had. For some businesses with enough latitude and variation, having their own platforms make sense but for most of the other businesses, going with a 3rd party platform is a prudent solution.

If your business deals with education and training, or is an events company, you can now explore the option of taking them to an online platform. Due to the COVID-19 crisis, many of these companies did not have much of a choice but go to an online platform.

Another prime example is Netflix that morphed from being a DVD rental company to being one of the world's leading streaming service companies. With the advances in technology and wide access of viewers, Netflix has essentially disrupted the way the world has been watching TV forever. By providing, anytime content, anywhere, any device, Netflix has taken the whole TV experience to a new dimension. You no longer need to be shackled by local TV stations, or channels, nor do you need to be restricted by timings of the program. And this has completely unleashed a new way of thinking and behaving. Now, you do not have to wait for Wednesday 9 o'clock for a prime time serial. You can now watch it whenever you want to. Not just that, you can binge watch and see the whole series in one night. And the best thing is that you are not interrupted with TV commercials every

10 minutes in the show.

From a technology perspective, Netflix uses big data analytics, data science, IoT, artificial intelligence, cloud computing and internet to bring their streaming services to people across the globe. Netflix is a great example on how a company moved from a brick-&-mortar business to a completely digital business.

Another example is that of cloud-based-services. By taking your product, software, or service to the cloud you can increase the ease of access and make it scalable. On top, to lure additional customers, you can offer free services, subscription based, or pay-as-you-go models to give you an extra edge to your business. A software business can create a cloud version that people can use from anywhere, any time as well as implement without the need of a CD/DVD or assisted implementation. Similarly, educational and consulting companies can put their material on the cloud that can be easily accessed and downloaded.

Value-Chain Network Collaboration

In this category, you look at the complete value-chain of an industry. It would start from the origination which can be farmers in case of agriculture, mines in case of metal and cattle-farms in case of meat and dairy. At the other end is the end consumer, the people who will ultimately use the product or businesses that would use the product. These value-chains include your suppliers, partners, customers as well as network collaborators, shipping and logistics companies, primary producers, marketeers, and many other parties.

By looking at the entire value-chain, it gives you a bigger perspective and highlights challenges that were not unearthed before. By going beyond your own supplier and customers, you also can unlock opportunities that would otherwise stay latent. With the advent of Blockchain, Internet-of-Things, online connectivity, ability to process big data and artificial intelligence, one can now easily exploit these opportunities. And many of them, can create conditions for direct competitive edge and get exponential growth.

This value-chain overview also, makes you begin to think of your customer's customer problems or supplier's supplier issues and challenges of intermediaries. And overall, provides an empathetic understanding of the various parties involved in the value-chain and start appreciating each other's contribution.

Issues related to fair-trade, source-of-origin, spare-part counterfeit, child labor issues and lost-in-transit challenges can be massively reduced by this digital approach.

With Blockchain and IoT, you can easily setup a transparent and trusted value-chain between multiple parties. Due to inherent security features of Blockchain, people can easily exchange information with each other in a tamper-proof environment. This can be a big plus if you operate in the healthcare industry, pharmaceuticals as well as industries like automotive, airline industries.

We have been involved in a couple of projects in this space. One of them dealt with the automotive industry. Value-chain of the automotive industry has multiple parties that include dealers, car manufacturers, contract manufacturers, local distribution centers, shipping companies, logistic providers as well as transporters. It is quite common for a dozen or more parties to be involved in any of the value-chains. Overarching view of the complete value-chain was always a mega issue. Companies are at the mercy of their suppliers or shipping companies on replenishing their inventories in a timely manner.

With the right digital technology, you can now create transparency across the complete chain with high accuracy and in real-time. Moreover, with Blockchain and IoT, you can create tamper-proof solutions to increase the confidence on the chain. Multiple parties can now work collaboratively to solve issues rather than engaging in a blame game as used to happen in the past.

Also, by providing real time track-and-trace, companies can radically reduce their inventories but also, address the issues with frauds and counterfeits much more accurately.

This type of approach can easily be pursued in agricultural

supply chain, dairy farming, fishing, and food processing industries. We also see them being used in automotive, industrial, airlines as well as health-tech, pharmaceuticals, and primary healthcare as well.

Co-Creation

The third digital accelerator is Co-creation

What is digital co-creation?

It is when a non-native digital company A creates an alliance with a digital company B to develop a digital product for the customers of company A. It uses a symbiotic relationship between the two companies to create a win-win situation.

It is most effective in a stagnant market and old economy businesses where the profit margins are razor-thin with lots of competition from traditional players. Companies struggle to grow in these environments despite spending money and effort in boosting growth through various improvement and organic initiatives, and in many cases, it also involved expensive IT upgrades as well.

These companies would also, have tried to create their own digital projects and made their presence felt through social media and regular online presence but still struggled to grow their business.

In other words, these companies are caught between a rock and a hard place. Breaking existing market shackles is not only difficult but is largely considered impossible.

This is when you need to actually think outside the box. And this is where Digital Co-creation comes into play.

The issues described usually stem from archaic policies, stiff regulations, and mind blocks. That is why, a fresh thinking is required.

Let us start with looking at your internal initiatives. As they did not yield the desired result, it is time to look beyond them and, in this case, look outside your company.

Secondly, do not look at your competition. Remember, you

operate in a highly competitive market. Chances are that they are also facing a similar dilemma. And if they seem to have a certain competitive advantage, they will protect that secret with their lives.

Third, you need to explore a huge array of ideas to stimulate your thinking.

Fourth, you cannot start from scratch with a product. You are not a startup business and you should not think that you can be one. Instead you should explore early-stage products or services that you can help develop further and scale. You need products that have gone through an initial exposure. This will prevent you from analysis-paralysis that seem to plague many innovations in corporate organizations and even mid-market businesses.

And the last one is that you potentially need an external partner with whom you can collaboratively, create your new product. This new partner not only brings you an outsider's perspective for your company, if the partner is from a startup, then you also get the entrepreneurship and the growth hunger of early stage companies. As you are operating in a stagnant market, and you need a digital product, your best bet is to go with a late-seed digital startup. With this company, you can explore and co-create the digital product that you were looking for.

This will create a true symbiotic partnership with a win-win configuration. You get a digital product by which you will be able to connect with your existing customers as well as new prospects, and increase your revenue. For the start-up, they will get investment backing and an existing customer base that they can readily deploy to. A true win-win in spirit as well as in practice.

Since this is a new concept, there are a few notable examples. However, each of them has disrupted the thinking and had a considerable growth.

Our co-creation examples are based on digital wearables like Fitbits and medical bracelets, which created a product for an insurance company, By using smartphone cameras and using it for cardiovascular and diabetes checks, and connecting them with Fitbit and medical bracelets, these companies created apps that are now quite popular and widely used in the community, going way beyond their customer base.

By going beyond your company's capabilities and looking outside for inspiration and partnership, you open up a wonderful world full of opportunities.

One point that I must highlight is that, while there is similarity between joint-ventures and co-creation, there also clear differences as well. Distinct separation of expectation of involved parties makes it ideal for companies to get into partnership. Second is non-exclusivity as it keeps the entrepreneurship of the start-ups in place. Third is financial maturity for both parties, for startups on how to judiciously use the invested capital and for the main company to keep a tab on returns on their investment. These are just a few critical differences amongst several others.

Magic happens, when you realize the strength of each other and play to it. In today's digital era, most companies will struggle to get digital capabilities. And that's why, digital co-creation can be a phenomenal option to pursue for your business.

Social Influence

The fourth accelerator is social influence where companies use social media to influence their existing customers as well as prospects and non-customers. Instead of just advertising their product features, companies try to interact with their users and get a deeper understanding of their behavior. What do they think, how do they interact on online social media, how do they interact with friends, how do they respond to digital marketing, product videos, websites, pop-ups and myriads of other items of interest are reviewed by companies.

Sometimes, the actual post made by companies have nothing in common with their product or services. Yet, these posts can create lasting impressions and much stronger brand recollection than their own product-feature posts.

Heineken created a video in which they showed two people

with politically opposing views talking with each other. None of Heineken products featured ever in the video except for their logo. This post went viral. And it created a lasting impression. And now whenever people recollect that video, they think Heineken. Clever proxy advertising, isn't it?

Social media influence has become a regular occurrence in elections across the globe. Micro-niche targeted messaging is now rampant across the globe during elections. It is not just about American politics but world over politicians are using these techniques.

Platforms like Facebook, Instagram, YouTube, LinkedIn, and Twitter are used for social influence due to their large user base.

Social media has also given rise to a new group of individuals called influencers. This group of people post contents as blogs, vlogs, podcasts, and videos. They write about food, restaurants, hotels, travel, technical gadgets, and various other things. They create YouTube videos and share their opinions about products, services, and experiences. Due to their candid and largely relatable opinions, they tend to create a big fan base. They are not celebrities, but they have thousands of followers on social media. And posts made by them often get millions of views. With a strong fan base and huge number of views, they are in a perfect position to endorse 3rd party products as well as bias people's views by their own opinions.

When a vlogger endorses a restaurant or a hotel and shares their own experiences, the demand for these places go up dramatically. Of course, the restaurant or the hotel is more than happy with the patronage they receive. Sometimes they pay to invite influencers to endorse their facilities. This is called influencer marketing.

There are multiple ways that companies are using social media to influence the market. Being on a digital platform and online presence, is giving them new techniques to influence the market like never seen before.

This is probably the easiest accelerator that a company can adopt and get exponential growth.

Digital Marketing

This accelerator is about marketing through digital channels to create awareness of your services and products in the market.

In the past, marketing was more of an art rather than a science. People used to spend huge amounts on marketing campaigns but struggled to get tangible data. They would keep their fingers crossed till they saw a positive revenue impact.

Now, users are creating digital footprints with every single interaction, and these digital footprints are generating significant amounts of data. This data can be studied and analyzed, and accordingly, businesses can create targeted marketing.

As mentioned in prior chapters, AIDA (Attention-Interest-Desire-Action) model is now the new favorite of digital marketeers. They can create sophisticated digital marketing funnel.

Using these digital funnels, companies create marketing campaign and release it on multiple channels. These channels can be social media platforms, emails, websites, or 3rd party enabling platforms like Eventbrite, HubSpot, and other apps.

Your average user is likely to interact with your campaign on more than one channel. They may read your email through their smartphone app. They may access your website on their desktops, and they may take actions by registering to events through Facebook, LinkedIn, or Eventbrite.

The moment campaign hits the market, and you have initiated the attention phase of AIDA, you start getting data about user interactions. This helps you to fine-tune or alter your marketing campaign accordingly.

There is a test called "5 second test". Research indicates that when users visit a new website, and if their interest is not piqued within 5 seconds, they move on to another website. That is why, many marketeers play with the headlines to figure out what messaging make users stay and what messaging loses them. This type of insight can give you a tremendous competitive edge over your competition.

Another interesting point is that unlike in the past when if one of your campaign went down badly, companies needed to spend thousands for damage control. But with digital platforms and artificial intelligence, and agile responses by UX (User eXperience) teams can prevent the glass from breaking. Companies like Amazon and Uber extensively use these dynamic decisions.

With the right funnel, digital marketing techniques and targeted marketing, you can drive deeper understanding about your users and increase your purchase conversion significantly.

Market Intelligence

The sixth accelerator is market intelligence. Internet ushered in the information age. Huge amounts of information are now available online. In fact, the volume is so huge that people now have issues on how to extract useful and intelligent information from the gargantuan pile of search results. You can now type in virtually any combination of a couple of words in google, and you are likely to get millions of records from the search result.

But how much of the available information can be actively used? How much relevance does these search results have? Many a times, you may need to synthesize information from several sources to create a meaningful understanding.

While Google and other search engines are constantly striving to improve their algorithms, we now see new types of companies emerging that are trying to address this issue. By using AI, they have created clever algorithms that can create insightful market intelligence.

Whether you are looking for potential buyers or trends in an industry, or you are exploring market dynamics, these specialized companies scour the internet and create high-impact reports.

This can be an extremely powerful tool when companies want to expand beyond their region, look for expanding their customer base, look at new ways to market their products and in some cases, even explore options of M&A (mergers and acquisitions) transaction.

With major educational institutes, libraries, patent agencies and other organizations opening their knowledge repository, there is plenty of structured information and primary research now available on the internet. With clever algorithm, artificial intelligence, and some good analytics, you can create market intelligence that can provide you with a huge competitive edge.

This digital technique is widely used in market research companies, event management companies as well as banks, financial institutes, consulting companies, analytics, and market intelligence. The outcome can be an industry report, the information can support organizing specialized business events and be the content of due diligence work in alliances and acquisitions.

Knowledge Marketing

This accelerator is probably one of the most undervalued of the entire set. This is where a company uses its knowledge and IP (intellectual property) base to attract potential buyers.

While knowledge marketing has significant similarity with content marketing, and many people would consider them to be the same, I would like to call out a couple of fundamental differences. Knowledge marketing can be categorized as specialized content marketing.

One of the key differences of knowledge marketing is that you use your own experience or provide your descriptive narrative about a topic. You can share your own methodology and framework or demonstrate your adeptness where you use strategic frames and techniques in designing your solutions.

In content management on the other side, it may be a blog or an article on a topic that is shared. Often, these articles are written by 3rd party writers vis-à-vis your own.

But the other crucial difference is that knowledge marketing is a form of an in-bound marketing. People after reading your article, viewing your videos, or listening to your podcasts would come to you rather than you going after them. It is pull-marketing form versus push-marketing that is the central tenet of content marketing.

So, how does pull marketing help? When people come to you or visit your website, that person already has qualified you as a potential provider of solution to their problems. You do not have to spend hours in creating marketing material or try to convince multiple people about your product. Instead you can focus your energy on creating a constructive conversation with the person. Another massive advantage of inbound marketing is that people end up paying a premium for your services.

Knowledge marketing can be a huge asset for knowledge-centric companies. These would include market research companies, consulting firms, educational and training companies, law firms and the likes.

Knowledge marketing can be exercised through multiple channels. You can write blogs, white-papers, and articles. You can create educational and experience-based videos. You can host subject specific events. You can create podcasts. And one of the most effective tools would be through writing books.

By sharing your own knowledge and experience, you create instant credibility as well as connection with the users based on relevance. You build trust with your consumers and more importantly, by sharing a little bit from your knowledge repository you create huge lead pipeline for your business.

Digitally Altered Business Models

The last part is not really an independent accelerator but a collection of several techniques that include digital centric business models.

First example is free-as-a-service or Freemium. In free-as-a-service, companies offer services partly or fully for free. This is used as a marketing tool to attract potential buyers. In freemium model, some part of services or products are made available for free, or the services are made available for free for a period referred to as a trial-period. Online apps, educational content, training, online magazines, software, and many other product companies use this approach.

Second category of specialized business model is centered around crowdsourcing user feedback and reviews. Companies like Amazon, TripAdvisor, Airbnb, and Uber use user reviews as a core pillar of their business. The entire collection and facilitation of user reviews is managed on an online platform.

Another category would be industry disruptors. Online banks are coming up fast. They offer 100% of their services online. You no longer must visit a branch, but you can conduct all your transactions being in the comfort of your homes. Moreover, the service charges are a lot lower than your high-street banks. These disruptors are taking old-economy businesses head-on and challenging all the rules, traditions, bureaucracy, and regulations. Revolut and Bunq are prime examples. All you need is a passport to open a bank account. And with that you can also get a standard industry recognized bank card. You no longer must make an appointment and go to a physical bank branch, ever!

So, this is an overview of eight digital accelerators. I can promise you one thing. If any one of these accelerators are deployed properly, any one of them can create exponential growth for most businesses. And, much more than what you can get through conventional approaches for sure.

◆ ◆ ◆

Checklist 5: Digital Examples For Ideation

You have read about the 8 digital accelerators. Now, you should use this set of questions to explore which accelerators can be relevant for your organization.

1. How many of these digital accelerators can be applied to your organization?

2. Which one of the innovative digital levers do you think will create the most impact?

3. Which one of the innovative digital levers can be adopted most easily?

4. What are some of the benefits that can be realized very quickly, and which ones will take time?

5. What hindrances are likely to surface if you want to adopt any of these accelerators?

6. What sort of change in management thinking would be required to pursue these accelerators?

7. What is the likely result if you do not adopt these accelerators and your competition adopts them?

CLOSING REMARKS

We have gone through a lot of details on how digital technology can provide you with huge opportunities to grow in this book. All companies must become technology companies in the coming decade for survival. Whether they create digital products or services, or use enabling technologies to promote and support their physical products, software or services, every company will need a strong digital backbone.

You have also seen with the digital adoption framework (DAF) how you can structurally go about adopting different digital applications that are relevant for your business.

As we come towards the end of the book, I would like to share some thoughts.

Diversity Of Digital Elements

It is not enough to go with the single digital element approach. With single elements, digital adoption stays peripheral at best. By introducing artificial intelligence-based recruitment engines or a few social media handles, you will not be able to unlock the real advantages of digital technology. There is a true amplification of power through the ripple effect of leveraging multiple digital approaches.

Digital Savvy Leadership

Digital adoption is not for the fainthearted. While it starts with technology, the real benefit is extracted when you unleash functional power of digital technologies to resolve most painful business problems. Not only would your teams need good understanding about the involved technologies, there is a significant amount of change management and leadership drive that is a prerequisite for successful digital adoption. Your digitally savvy leadership should not only understand the power of technology but also acutely understand the problem areas of your business and where these technologies can be used. And the cultural change that needs to be brought about in your organization. They must lead this initiative from the front.

Culture Of Experiment

For any successful digital adoption, a company must have a strong culture of experimentation. If you have been in a risk-averse business, then you must take steps to become an innovative company. Instead of focusing on desktop business cases, and death by PowerPoint presentations, you need to cultivate a culture where everybody is free to share ideas and participate in experiments. This culture needs to permeate across different layers of your company. It is no longer considered a privilege for a few. Your company needs to foster open culture where people should be able to voice their opinions without the fear of any retribution.

Agile

When you embark on a digital adoption journey, there are a lot of uncertainties that exist. During your journey you will discover new things that will require you to modify and course correct your direction. All of this cannot be predicted or estimated upfront. To have lengthy preparations for creating project plans or business cases, is not practical. Rapid innovation and large-scale experimentation would need a certain degree of agility in the organization. Given the usual circumstances, we strongly recommend agile and lean startup methods to be deployed during digital adoption journey. Managing through user stories and sprints will significantly improve your chances of a successful adoption.

Engage Experts

There are several components of digital technology where you will need specific expertise to implement. In the past, companies would invest heavily in creating this expertise in-house. With rapid technology changes and the need for surge expert resources for a short duration, it is recommended that you get this expertise from outside. Since these resource are expensive, with gig economy, it is going to be more convenient to engage them on short-term gigs rather than long term employments.

Every business has their own unique requirements. At the same time many of these requirements have similar foundational issues. My idea with this book is to provide you with a structured thinking approach on how to leverage the right technology elements that can help your business grow. I can fully assure you that you will have a successful digital adoption journey as the framework distributes your risks and creates a lot more opportunities.

Finally, every new business concept and framework only gets better with usage and application. That is why, I will be keen to hear from you about your experiences and learning with using the knowledge shared with you in advice this book. And of course, do send your questions and enquiries to me to enrich the knowledge base.

ACKNOWLEDGEMENT

I would like to thank my wife and my editor, Devyani Sen who stood by me during this crazy phase of writing this book. She helped me distill through thousands of ideas into a coherent set for this book.

I would like to thank my daughter, Anahita and son, Rishaan who withstood my idiosyncrasies, helped me ideate and shown maturity beyond their years.

I would like to thank Lakshmi Venkat Vemuganti, Nupur Chakraborty, Hutton Henry, Dr. Jaijit Bhattacharya and Christopher C Doyle who have allowed me to pick their brains at all hours of the day.

I would like to thank Andy Buyting, Nico Eggert, Adi Mazor Kario, Paul Bessems, Eduardo Gomez Ruiz, Ajit Kumar Amit, Nitin Kumar, Monisha Ghosh, Ragav Jagannathan and Amlan Sen for sharing their experiences and examples to enrich this book.
I would also like to thank my friends and colleagues, and you know who you are. You have supported me and helped me shape the person that I am today.

And finally, I would like to thank my family and my in-laws who have stood by me through the highs and lows of my life.

◆ ◆ ◆